MW00834793

PREDICTING THE MARKETS

The Yield Curve: What Is It Really Predicting?

Edward Yardeni
Melissa Tagg

YRI PRESS

Edward Yardeni is President of Yardeni Research, Inc.
Melissa Tagg is a Senior Economist at the firm.

Predicting the Markets Topical Study #1:
The Yield Curve: What Is It Really Predicting?

ISBN: 978-1-948025-02-7 (eBook)
ISBN: 978-1-948025-03-4 (paperback)

Published by YRI Press, a division of Yardeni Research, Inc.
68 Wheatley Road, Suite 1100
Brookville, New York 11545

Contact us: **requests@yardeni.com**

A Note to Readers

These Topical Studies examine issues
discussed in my book, *Predicting the Markets:
A Professional Autobiography* (2018), in greater
detail and on a more current basis.

The charts included at the end
of this study were current as of May 2019.
Updates (in color) are available at
www.yardeni.com/studies

Institutional investors are welcome
to sign up for our research service on a
four-week complimentary basis at
www.yardeni.com/trial-registration

Introduction

Is the flattening yield curve predicting a recession? In our opinion, the yield curve, first and foremost, predicts the Fed policy cycle rather than the business cycle. Our research confirms this conclusion, as does a recent Fed study. More specifically, inverted yield curves don't cause recessions. Instead, they provide a useful market signal that monetary policy is too tight and risks triggering a financial crisis, which can quickly turn into a credit crunch causing a recession. If so, then the Fed's recent decision to be patient and pause its rate-hiking may reduce the chances of a recession.

In my recent book *Predicting the Markets*, I wrote: "The Yield Curve Model is based on investors' expectations of how the Fed will respond to inflation. It is more practical for predicting interest rates than is the Inflation Premium Model. It makes sense that the federal funds rate depends mostly on the Fed's inflation outlook, and that all the other yields to the right of this rate on the yield curve are determined by investors' expectations for the Fed policy cycle." (See Appendix 1: Primer on the Yield Curve for a fuller excerpt on this subject from my book.)

Subsequent research by Melissa and myself has confirmed this conclusion, as discussed in this Topical Study. More specifically, after studying the relationship between the yield curve and the monetary, credit, and business cycles, we have concluded that it is credit crunches—not an inverted yield curve and not aging economic expansions—that cause recessions. The yield curve is just keeping score on how the Fed is reacting to and influencing these cycles. So why do inverted yield curves have such a good track record of calling recessions, and could it be different this time?

On Friday, March 22, 2019, the stock market freaked out when the yield curve inverted (Fig. 1). The yield curve did so ever so slightly, as the 10-year US Treasury bond yield fell to 2.44%, just 2 basis points below the three-month T-bill rate; but it was still 7 basis points above the federal funds rate (Fig. 2). That raised fears of a recession, reinforced by some weak Purchasing Managers Index data out of Europe (Fig. 3).

We didn't freak out because we aren't convinced that the fixed-income markets are unambiguously signaling that a recession is coming, especially given the narrowing of credit-quality yield spreads. For example, the yield spread between the high-yield and the 10-year Treasury bond continued to narrow from a recent peak of 530 basis points on January 3 to 379 basis points on Thursday, March 21 (Fig. 4).

During 2018, there was lots of chatter about the 10-year bond yield possibly rising toward 4.00% or even 5.00% because of Trump's deficit-widening tax cuts and the Fed's anticipated "normalization" of monetary policy. Some commentators warned that when the yield rose above 3.00%, that could spell trouble for stocks.

The yield moved decisively above that level on September 18, 2018 (Fig. 5). A sharp correction in the stock market ensued, with the S&P 500 dropping 19.8% from September 20 through December 24. Now that the bond yield is down around 2.40%, the new worry is that such a low yield might be a bad omen for the economy and stocks, especially since the yield curve has flattened so much since late last year. In what follows, we consider some reasons not to freak out about the yield curve.

Leading Indicator

The yield-curve spread between the 10-year US Treasury bond yield and the federal funds rate is only one of the 10 components of the monthly Index of Leading Economic Indicators (LEI). The index is compiled by The Conference Board, which added the difference between the 10-year Treasury note yield and the federal funds rate to the LEI in 1996 in a revision that also deleted two components of the LEI, the change in the index of sensitive materials prices and the change in manufacturers' unfilled orders for durable goods.[1] This spread fell to two basis points on March 28, remaining slightly positive. Though it is down from last year's peak of about 150 basis points in February, it doesn't actually weigh on the LEI until it turns negative.

The LEI edged up 0.2% during February (Fig. 6). It's been essentially flat for the past five months, though it is still on an uptrend. At a record high is the Index of Coincident Economic Indicators. It was up 2.5% year over year during February, suggesting that real GDP is growing by at least that pace (Fig. 7).

Prior to the last seven recessions, the yield curve inverted with a lead time of 55 weeks on average, in a range of 40-77 weeks (Fig. 8). It gave a few false, though short-lived, signals along the way, during the 1980s and 1990s. For example, during the longest economic expansion to date, the yield curve turned negative a couple of times in 1995 and again in 1998. The recession started a few years later, in March 2001. The signal seems to

---

1 See The New Treatment of the Yield Spread in the TCB Composite Index of Leading Indicators, Conference Board 2005 report: "In conclusion, the transition to using the cumulative yield spread is supported by both theoretical reasons and empirical evidence. Theory suggests that the yield curve should contribute negatively to the LEI when it inverts, not just when it is declining. The cumulative yield spread successfully captures this property. In practice, the cumulative yield spread is smoother and is a better leading indicator than its raw form.

work better as a recession indicator the longer the curve has been inverted. It hasn't been negative so far through early April.

The S&P 500 stock price index is also one of the 10 components of the LEI. Not surprisingly, therefore, the yield curve tends to start inverting at the same time as a bear market in stocks begins (Fig. 9). If the yield curve inverts more decisively and if the stock market heads lower, we might become concerned about an impending recession. We don't expect to have to do so anytime soon.

Monetary Policy Cycle

The yield curve tends to increasingly flatten, then invert during periods when the Fed is raising the federal funds rate (Fig. 10). That makes sense, since rising short-term rates increasingly raise the odds of a recession, which makes Treasury bonds increasingly attractive.

Just before the Fed starts lowering the federal funds rate is when the yield-curve spread is most negative; it starts moving toward positive territory as the Fed lowers interest rates faster than bond yields are falling. Once it starts ascending again, the yield curve's slope tends to steepen as the Fed stops lowering the federal funds rate and starts to slowly raise it again.

Where are we now in the monetary policy cycle? The tightening phase may be over for a while. This may be a pause before the Fed moves again later this year or not until next year, and with only one rate hike, if the Fed's latest forecast is on the money (though its forecasts haven't been in quite some time). Or, the Fed may be in the early phase of another easing cycle. Either way, the yield-curve spread may stay right around zero for a while, without clearly signaling a recession as widely feared.

Boom-Bust Cycle

In the past, the Fed would raise the federal funds rate during economic booms to stop an acceleration of inflation. Fed officials did so aggressively, perhaps in no small measure to shore up their credibility as inflation fighters. Tightening monetary conditions often triggered a credit crunch—particularly during the 1960s and 1970s, when interest-rate ceilings on bank deposits were set by Regulation Q—as even the credit-worthiest of borrowers found that bankers were less willing and able to lend them money.

Sensing this mounting stress in the credit markets and expecting the credit crunch to cause a recession and a bear market in stocks, investors would pile into

Treasury bonds. The yield curve inverted, accurately anticipating the increasingly obvious chain of events that ensued—i.e., rising interest rates triggered a credit crisis, which led to a widespread credit crunch and a recession, causing the Fed to lower short-term interest rates.

So how can we explain the flattening of the yield curve during the current business cycle? Inflation remains relatively subdued, around the Fed's 2.0% target (measured by the personal consumption expenditures deflator excluding food and energy on a year-over-year basis). It rose to that pace during May 2018 for the first time since the target was explicitly established by the Fed on January 25, 2012 (Fig. 11).

The Fed has gradually been raising the federal funds rate since late 2015, yet few critics charge that the Fed is behind the curve on inflation and needs to raise interest rates more aggressively. The economy is performing well, but there are few signs of an inflationary boom or major speculative excesses that require a more forceful normalization of monetary policy, which might trigger a recession.

Credit Cycle

Notwithstanding the previous false alarms (including the most recent flattening of the yield curve), the question of why the yield curve has consistently inverted prior to recessions remains. One widely held view is that banks stop lending when the rates they pay in the money markets on their deposits and their borrowings exceed the rates they charge on the loans they make to businesses and households. So an inverted yield curve heralds a credit crunch, which inevitably causes a recession.

In a December 5, 2018 post on Eaton Vance's Advisory Blog, Andrew Szczurowski convincingly argued that "the market is looking at the wrong curve. It's not an inverted 2s-10s, or 2s-30s, or 2s-5s curve that matters. What really matters, in my mind, is what is happening to the curves at banks." He observed: "At the same time, the rates banks are charging for a mortgage are up 150 basis points from their lows. This is the first hiking cycle where banks' margins are actually increasing as the Fed is hiking rates. The reason being, they aren't paying their depositors much more today than they were over the past few years."

So what really matters is the net interest margin of the banks. Consider the following:

- **Net interest margin.** The widely held notion that a flat or an inverted yield curve causes banks to stop lending doesn't make much sense. The net interest margin, which is reported quarterly by the Federal Deposit Insurance Corporation (FDIC), has been solidly positive for banks since the start of the data in 1984 (Fig. 12). The net interest income of FDIC-insured institutions rose to a record $140.2 billion during the fourth quarter of 2018.

- **Charge-offs and dividends.** There's no sign of distress, or even stress, in the FDIC data. Net charge-offs have been relatively stable around $10 billion per quarter for the past few years. Provisions for loan losses have matched the charge-offs. Cash dividends rose to a record $52.7 billion during the fourth quarter of 2018.

- **Business loans.** Inverted yield curves tend to be associated with periods of monetary tightening, which often trigger financial crises and credit crunches. There's certainly no credit crunch today. Short-term business credit rose to a record high during the March 13 week (Fig. 13).

Global Perspective

The US bond market has become more globalized. It is not driven exclusively by the US business cycle and Fed policies. The rate of inflation is low not only in the US but also around the world. However, evidence of an economic slowdown is more apparent in other parts of the world than in the US.

The European Central Bank (ECB) first lowered its official deposit rate to below zero on June 5, 2014. The Bank of Japan (BOJ) lowered its official rate to below zero on January 29, 2016. Those rates, which remain slightly below zero, have reduced 10-year government bond yields to around zero in both Germany and Japan since 2015.

The negative-interest-rate policies of the ECB and BOJ have been major contributors to the flattening of the US yield curve, in our opinion. Low global yields make comparable US Treasury bonds attractive to investors, especially when investors turn to a risk-off mode (Fig. 14). Perhaps the flattening of the US yield curve reflects that the world is flat.

Bond Vigilantes

There's a close correlation between the 10-year US Treasury bond yield and the growth rate of nominal GDP on a year-over-year basis (Fig. 15 and Fig. 16). The former has always traded in the same neighborhood as the latter. In my book, I call this relationship the "Bond Vigilantes Model." The challenge is to explain why the two variables aren't identical at any point or period in time. Nominal GDP rose 5.2% during the fourth quarter of 2018. Yet the US bond yield is below 3.00%.

During the 1960s and 1970s, bond investors weren't very vigilant about inflation and consistently purchased bonds at yields below the nominal GDP growth rate. They suffered significant losses. During the 1980s and 1990s, they turned into inflation- fighting Bond Vigilantes, keeping bond yields above nominal GDP growth.

Since the Great Recession of 2008, the Wild Bunch has been held in check by the major central banks, which have had near-zero interest-rate policies and massive quantitative easing programs that have swelled their balance sheets with bonds. Meanwhile, powerful structural forces have kept a lid on inflation—all the more reason for the Bond Vigilantes to have relaxed their guard.

As noted above, a global perspective certainly helps to explain why the US bond yield is well below nominal GDP growth. So this time may be different than in the past for the bond market, which has become more globalized and influenced by the monetary policies not only of the Fed but also of the other major central banks.

Fed Study

According to a July 2018 Fed note, the probability of a recession at that time was around 14% based on a yield-curve model. However, a February 2019 update study reported that the odds had risen to 50%. That recession warning might have contributed to the Fed's remarkable pivot from a hawkish to a dovish stance on monetary policy since the start of this year. However, the warning was hedged considerably. Let's have a close look at this important study:

- **Original note.** The minutes of the June 12-13 FOMC meeting offered a reason not to worry about the flattening yield curve. During the meeting, Fed staff presented an alternative "indicator of the likelihood of recession" based on research explained in a 6/28 FEDS Notes titled "(Don't Fear) The Yield Curve" by two Fed economists, Eric C. Engstrom and Steven A.

Sharpe. In brief, they questioned why a "long-term spread" between the 10-year and 2-year Treasury notes should have much power to predict imminent recessions. As an alternative, they devised a 0- to 6-quarter "near-term forward spread" based on the spread between the current level of the federal funds rate and the expected federal funds rate several quarters ahead, derived from futures market prices (Fig. 17).

The note's authors stressed that the long-term spread reflects the near-term spread, and the near-term spread, they argued, makes more sense as an indicator of a near-term recession, i.e., one that is expected to occur within the next few quarters. They also observe that an inversion of either yield spread does not mean that the spread causes recessions.

Their conclusion back then was that "the market is putting fairly low odds on a rate cut over the next four quarters," i.e., 14.1% (Fig. 18). "Unlike far-term yield spreads, the near-term forward spread has not been trending down in recent years, and survey-based measures of longer-term expectations for short term interest rates show no sign of an expected inversion."

- **Updated study.** The updated, February 2019 version of the Fed study is titled: "The Near-Term Forward Yield Spread as a Leading Indicator: A Less Distorted

Mirror." Engstrom and Sharpe observed that their near-term spread "can be interpreted as a measure of the market's expectations for the near-term trajectory of conventional monetary policy rates."

In addition, they reported: "Its predictive power suggests that, when market participants expected—and priced in—a monetary policy easing over the subsequent year and a half, a recession" was likely forthcoming. The near-term spread "predicts four-quarter GDP growth with greater accuracy than survey consensus forecasts. Furthermore, "it has substantial predictive power for stock returns," found the Fed economists. In contrast, yields on bonds "maturing beyond 6-8 quarters are shown to have no added value for forecasting either recessions, GDP growth, or stock returns."

- **A highly hedged warning.** Buried on page 7 of the new study is a warning that the probability of a recession based on the near-term forward yield spread had increased significantly since the original study was done about a year ago: "As of the end of the sample period in early 2019 (and the time of this writing), the near-term forward spreads forecasted a substantially elevated probability of a recession."

Indeed, Figure 3 in the study clearly shows that it jumped to 50% (based on limited first-quarter 2019 data, available only through January). Interestingly, this important update wasn't mentioned in the summary paragraph at the beginning of the study. In any event, the charts in the paper showed that the odds of a recession jump most significantly when the near-term forward spread is markedly below zero, which it was not as of the most recent analysis.

Accordingly, we're not freaking out about an impending recession. We are focusing on the idea I discussed in my book, and confirmed in the Fed study, that the yield curve first and foremost is predicting the outlook for monetary policy, not for recession. For example, the Fed paper noted that "the near-term forward spread would tend to turn negative when investors decide that the Fed is likely to soon switch from a tightening to an easing stance."

As noted above, the yield-curve spread tends to narrow during periods when the Fed is raising the federal funds rate. It tends to bottom and then widen when the Fed starts to lower interest rates. It just so happens that past recessions occurred after the yield curve inverted, i.e., at the tail end of monetary tightening cycles.

It might be different this time, if the Fed has paused on a timely basis from raising interest rates any further, thus reducing the chances of a recession. After all, there's no need to overdo tightening given that inflation and speculative excesses remain subdued. In the past, Fed tightening (not inverted yield curves that coincided with tightening) led to financial crises, which morphed into widespread credit crunches, resulting in recessions (Fig. 19).

Hence, our conclusion that it is credit crunches that cause recessions, not inverted yield curves and not aging expansions.

- **False positive signal.** Drawing parallels between monetary policy in 1998 and today, Engstrom's and Sharpe's paper stated: "The most prominent false positive during our sample came with the anticipated easing triggered by the spread of the Asian financial crises in 1998, which did not result in a recession in the U.S. It is not hard to imagine that similar scenarios could generate additional false positives in the future. The near-inversion of the near term forward spread at the end of 2018 seems to have been associated with market perceptions of significant risks to the global economic outlook, including the threat of escalating trade disputes. Whether those risks manifest in a recession remains to be seen." More reason to believe the yield curve's credibility as a reliable recession predictor has been overblown.

Predicting the Fed

As explained above, the yield-curve spread first and foremost is predicting monetary policy. The Fed study confirms that point and convincingly observes that it makes more sense to focus on the shape of the yield curve over the next six quarters rather than over the next 10 years for insights into the fixed-income market's outlook for monetary policy. In this spirit, let's review the market's latest divinations:

- **Missing in action.** The Fed study notes: "We define the near-term forward spread on any given day as the difference between the implied interest rate expected on a three-month Treasury bill six quarters ahead and the current yield on a three- month Treasury bill."

  According to Haver Analytics (our data vendor): "We had been in touch with the Board about the 0-to-6 Quarter Forward Spread earlier this year and they had told us they calculated it using an internal fitted zero coupon curve in quarterly maturities. They only make annual maturities available now, so we cannot calculate."

- **The two-year yield curve.** So instead of trying to calculate the Fed study's near-term spread, we will focus on the 12-month forward futures for the federal funds rate, which is available daily (Fig. 20). The two-year US Treasury note yield tracks this series very closely, suggesting that it is also a good proxy for the market's prediction of the federal funds rate a year from now.

- **Pause prediction.** After all that work, the conclusion is obvious: The Fed isn't likely to be raising the federal funds rate over the next 12 months. On March 28, the 12-month forward rate was 2.05%, 33 basis points below the 2.38% mid-point of the federal funds rate target range. On the same day, the two-year Treasury note was 2.23%, 15 basis points below the mid-point.

  The Fed study suggests to us that the spread between the two-year Treasury yield and the federal funds rate may be the simplest way to track the fixed-income market's outlook for monetary policy over the next 52 weeks (Fig._21 and Fig. 22). Anyone can do this at home. But that doesn't mean that the market will be right, as evidenced by how wrong it turned out to be last year.

Bottom Line

The shape of the yield curve may provide useful market signals for Fed officials to consider when they are deciding on the course of monetary policy:

- **A widening yield-curve** suggests that the Fed can tighten monetary policy if necessary without risking a recession.
- **A flattening yield curve** suggests that the pace of rate-hiking should be slowed, while a flat yield curve might be a good signal for the Fed to pause tightening for a while.
- **An inverted yield curve** indicates that monetary conditions are too tight and that easing might be in order.

For now, we still don't see a significant risk of a recession on the horizon, especially since the FOMC recently switched from a gradual pace of rate hikes to a patient approach. The committee's decision in March to pause hiking the federal funds rate, possibly over the rest of this year, reduces the risks of a credit crunch and a recession. That's the current message from the yield curve.

Appendix 1

Primer on the Yield Curve
Reproduced from
Predicting the Markets: A Professional Autobiography
Edward Yardeni

THE YIELD CURVE Model is more fun and potentially more useful (and profitable) than the Inflation Premium Model. It posits that bond yields are determined by expectations for short-term interest rates over the maturity of the bond. These expectations are embedded in the "term structure of interest rates," as reflected in the shape of the yield curve.

The yield curve is simply a table showing the yield on various-maturity US Treasuries at any point in time. When shown as a chart at a point in time, it usually connects the market yields of the three-month, six- month, and 12-month Treasury bills, the two-year and five-year notes, and the 10-year and 30-year bonds at that time. The so-called "short end" of the yield curve tends to be very sensitive to actual and expected short-term changes in the federal funds rate. The "long end" of the curve can be more or less sensitive to such changes, depending on longer-term expectations for the federal funds rate.

The slope of the yield curve reflects the "term structure" of interest rates. Think of the 10-year yield as reflecting the current one-year bill rate and expectations for that rate over the next nine years. The one-year bill rate reflects the current six-month bill rate and expectations for the six-month bill rate six months from now. Of course, there are plenty of other combinations of shorter-term rates and expectations about them that are reflected in longer-term rates.

Over time, the overall slope of the yield curve is typically measured as the difference between the 10-year yield and the federal funds rate. As I observe in Chapter 5, this spread is one of the components of the Index of Leading Economic Indicators (LEI). Let's look at this business cycle indicator in the context of forecasting the interest-rate cycle:

- **An ascending yield curve** indicates that investors expect short-term interest rates to rise over time; they demand higher rates for tying their money up longer with long-maturing bonds. So a positive yield curve spread implies market expectations of rising interest rates.

- **A flat yield curve** suggests that investors expect short-term rates to remain stable for the future. For example, today's six-month Treasury bill rate should be the same as today's three-month Treasury bill rate if the latter is expected to be unchanged three months from now, and so on all along the maturity spectrum of the yield curve. At times, the Fed has raised the federal funds rate sharply, yet bond yields didn't rise as much as rates on bills and notes. Such flattening of the yield curve tended to happen when investors expected that the tightening of monetary policy was likely to cause a recession and bring down inflation.

- **An "inverted" yield curve** has a downward slope, suggesting that investors are scrambling to lock in longterm yields before they fall. The yield curve spread is negative. This typically happens when short- term rates soar above bond yields as the Fed tightens monetary policy to fight inflation. An inverted yield curve suggests that investors believe this will cause a recession, with short-term interest rates heading back down below bond yields. They expect locked-in yields to exceed the short-term interest rates during most of the investment horizon. The yield curve might then invert, with short-term rates rising above long-term rates as investors become more convinced that rising short-term rates will cause an economic downturn, prompting the Fed to yank the federal funds rate back down. Then, short-term rates will drop back below long-term rates, and the yield curve once again will signal better economic times ahead.

In the years prior to my career, the yield curve was a very useful tool for those forecasting the business cycle.

During the 1960s and 1970s, the financial markets were highly regulated. For example, the Fed's Regulation Q allowed the central bank to set ceilings on interest rates paid on deposits by commercial banks and by S&Ls. When the Fed raised the federal funds rate to slow the economy and bring down inflation, it all happened rapidly once money- market interest rates rose above the Regulation Q ceilings. That's because money poured out of deposits and into money-market instruments.

The process is called "disintermediation," as I note in previous chapters. Its consequence is a credit crunch, which [Henry] Kaufman well understood. Financial intermediaries facing deposit outflows would stop extending credit to consumers, homebuyers, and businesses. Kaufman believed that these credit crunches and the busts they caused were necessary from time to time to eliminate the financial excesses that always occur during booms.

From that perspective, Regulation Q was a very useful and effective way for the Fed to put an end to booms. However, banks hated disintermediation and the public hated credit crunches, so political pressure led to a wave of financial market deregulation. Regulation Q deposit ceilings were phased out from 1981 to 1986 by the Depository Institutions Deregulation and Monetary Control Act of 1980, as Chapters 1 and 8 discuss.

Nevertheless, the yield curve continued to work as a business-cycle indicator. The spread between the 10- year Treasury bond yield and the federal funds rate has been one of the components of the LEI since 1996. For many years, the index reflected the month-to-month changes in the spread. So if the spread widened, that would contribute positively to the LEI, pulling the index higher, and if it narrowed, the spread's contribution would be negative, pulling the index lower. During 2005, the spread's contribution was changed to put more weight on whether it was positive or negative. That way, the spread contributes positively (negatively) to LEI only when it is itself positive (negative), not when it rises (falls). The Conference Board, which compiles the LEI every month, cumulates the spread month by month.

Since the Great Recession of 2008, the Fed and other central banks have played a much bigger role in influencing bond yields. They've always had a big impact on the long end of the yield curve since they have a big influence on expectations about the course of short-term rates. What changed is that they started buying bonds often and in size through their various QE programs.

The credit markets clearly are very efficient and competitive. They are free markets and remain less regulated now than they were in the 1960s and 1970s. However, the central banks (a.k.a. "central monetary planners") have become the biggest buyers in the bond market in recent years. In other words, the free markets for credit are hardly free of the influence of the central banks. This means that the central banks may be distorting the viability of the yield curve as a business-cycle indicator.

Nevertheless, if and when the yield curve inverts again, it will still get my attention as a warning signal that something isn't right with the economy. Pessimistically inclined prognosticators undoubtedly will warn that a recession is imminent.

In this Yield Curve Model, inflation matters a great deal to markets because it matters to the central bank. Investors have learned to anticipate how the Fed's inflationary expectations might drive short-term interest rates, and to determine yields on bonds accordingly. So the measure of inflationary expectations deduced from the yield spread between the Treasury bond and the TIPS might very well reflect not only the expectations of borrowers and lenders but also their assessment of the expectations and the likely response of Fed officials! The data are very supportive of these relationships among inflation, the Fed policy cycle, and the bond yield.

The Fed policy cycle is easy to depict. Tightening occurs from a cyclical trough to a cyclical peak in the federal funds rate. Easing occurs between the peaks and the troughs. Not surprisingly, since 1960, tightening has occurred during periods of rising inflation, while easing has occurred during periods of falling inflation or relatively low and stable inflation. Sure enough, the yield curve spread tends to widen from its negative trough to its positive peak during the early stage of monetary easing. The yield curve spread tends to peak during the late stage of monetary easing. When monetary tightening begins, the spread falls, turning less positive and then going negative during the late stage of tightening.

The interest-rate forecasting models discussed above aren't mutually exclusive. All three are based on the premise that inflation is the main driver of interest rates; the flow of funds is a sideshow. Here's how they differ:

- **The Bond Vigilantes Model** relates the bond yield to the growth rate in nominal GDP, which reflects inflation as well as the real growth of the economy. The divergence between the nominal growth rate and the bond yield may very well be influenced by the inflationary expectations of investors as well as by their expectations for monetary policy.

- **The Inflation Premium Model** is based on the inflationary expectations of investors. In my opinion, it's not as useful to view the bond yield as some vague hypothetical real rate plus investors' inflation expectations, unless that mumbo jumbo is influencing Fed policymaking.

- **The Yield Curve Model** is based on investors' expectations of how the Fed will respond to inflation. It is more practical for predicting interest rates than is the Inflation Premium Model. It makes sense that the federal funds rate depends mostly on the Fed's inflation outlook, and that all the other yields to the right of this rate on the yield curve are determined by investors' expectations for the Fed policy cycle.

A Note to Readers

The charts included at the end
of this study were current as of May 2019.
Updates (in color) are available at
www.yardeni.com/studies

Institutional investors are welcome
to sign up for our research service on a
four-week complimentary basis at
www.yardeni.com/trial-registration

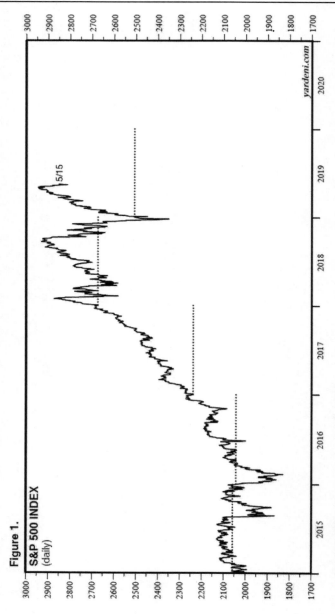

Figure 1.

S&P 500 INDEX
(daily)

5/15

yardeni.com

Note: Dotted lines show previous years' closing prices.
Source: Standard & Poor's.

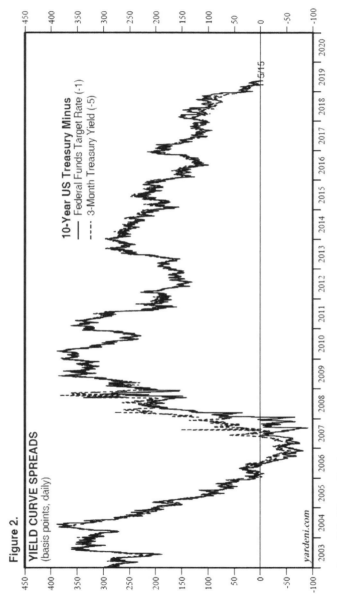

Figure 2.

YIELD CURVE SPREADS
(basis points, daily)

10-Year US Treasury Minus
—— Federal Funds Target Rate (-1)
---- 3-Month Treasury Yield (-5)

yardeni.com

Source: Federal Reserve Board

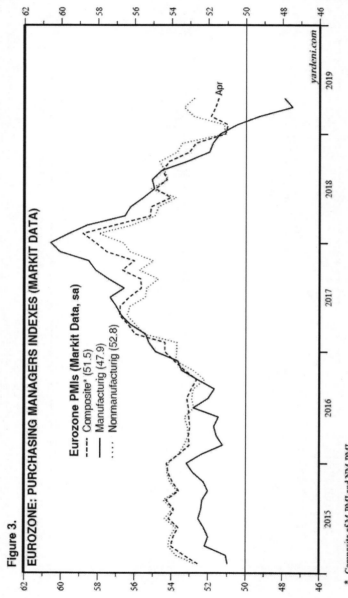

Figure 3.
EUROZONE: PURCHASING MANAGERS INDEXES (MARKIT DATA)

Eurozone PMIs (Markit Data, sa)
- - - - Composite* (51.5)
——— Manufacturig (47.9)
········· Nonmanufacturig (52.8)

yardeni.com

* Composite of M-PMI and NM-PMI
Source: Markit and Haver Analytics.

Figure 4.

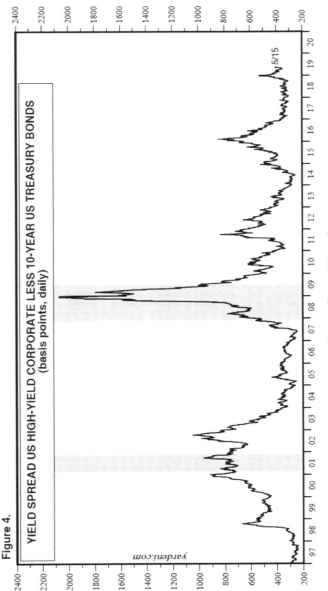

YIELD SPREAD US HIGH-YIELD CORPORATE LESS 10-YEAR US TREASURY BONDS
(basis points, daily)

Note: Shaded areas denote recessions according to the National Bureau of Economic Research.
Source: Bank of America Merrill Lynch and Federal Reserve Board

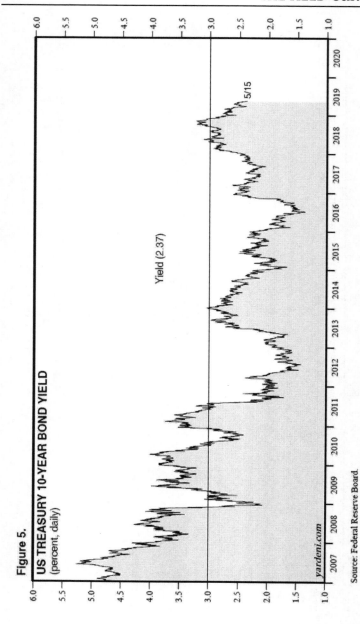

Figure 5.

US TREASURY 10-YEAR BOND YIELD
(percent, daily)

Yield (2.37)

5/15

yardeni.com

Source: Federal Reserve Board

Figure 6.

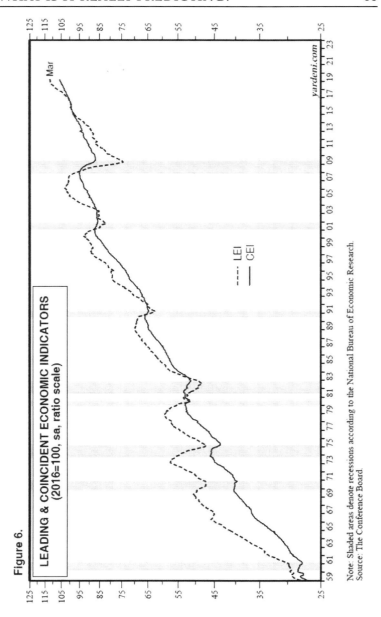

LEADING & COINCIDENT ECONOMIC INDICATORS
(2016=100, sa, ratio scale)

LEI

CEI

yardeni.com

Note: Shaded areas denote recessions according to the National Bureau of Economic Research.
Source: The Conference Board

Figure 7.

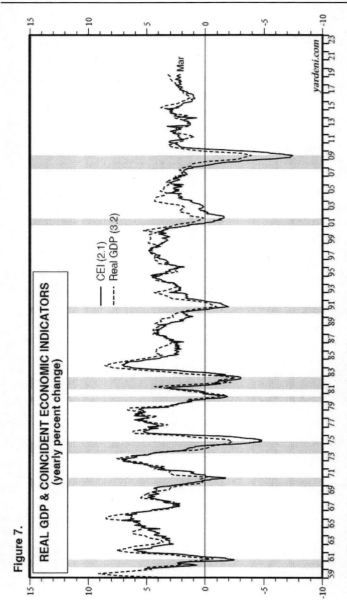

REAL GDP & COINCIDENT ECONOMIC INDICATORS
(yearly percent change)

CEI (2.1)
Real GDP (3.2)

Mar

yardeni.com

Note: Shaded areas denote recessions according to the National Bureau of Economic Research.
Source: Bureau of Economic Analysis and Conference Board.

Figure 8.

US YIELD CURVE* &
BUSINESS CYCLE
(basis points, weekly)

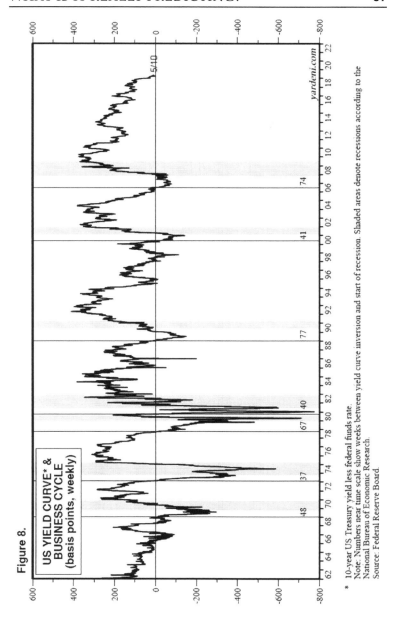

*   10-year US Treasury yield less federal funds rate.
    Note: Numbers near time scale show weeks between yield curve inversion and start of recession. Shaded areas denote recessions according to the
    National Bureau of Economic Research.
    Source: Federal Reserve Board

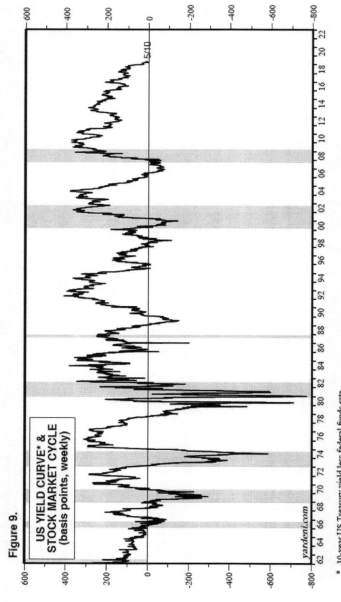

Figure 9.

US YIELD CURVE* &
STOCK MARKET CYCLE
(basis points, weekly)

yardeni.com

* 10-year US Treasury yield less federal funds rate.
Note: Shaded grey areas denote S&P 500 bear market declines of 20% or more. White areas show bull markets.
Source: Federal Reserve Board.

Figure 10.

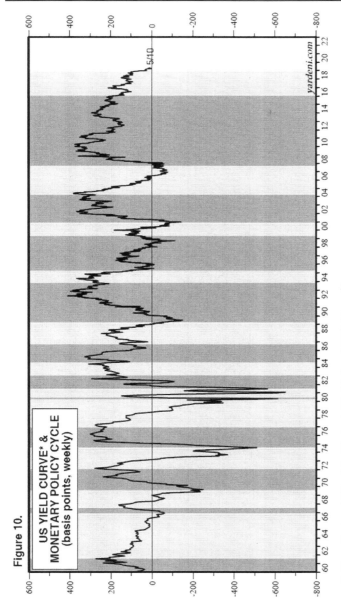

US YIELD CURVE* &
MONETARY POLICY CYCLE
(basis points, weekly)

5/10

yardeni.com

* 10-year Treasury yield less federal funds rate. Monthly through 1987, then weekly.
Note: Dark grey shaded areas denote periods of monetary easing between cyclical peaks and troughs in the federal funds rate. Light grey shaded areas denote
monetary tightening periods.
Source: Federal Reserve Board

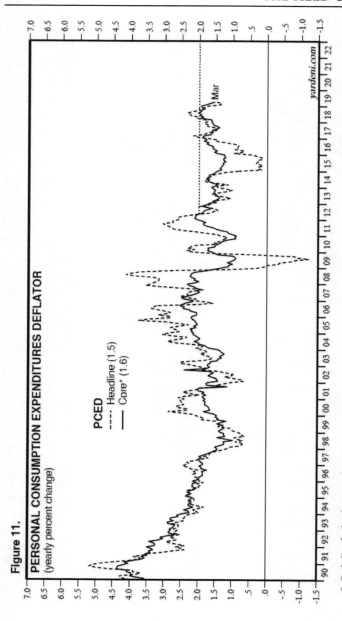

Figure 11.

PERSONAL CONSUMPTION EXPENDITURES DEFLATOR
(yearly percent change)

PCED
---- Headline (1.5)
—— Core* (1.6)

* Excluding food and energy prices.
Note: Dotted line is the Fed's official target set during January 2012.
Source: Bureau of Economic Analysis.

yardeni.com

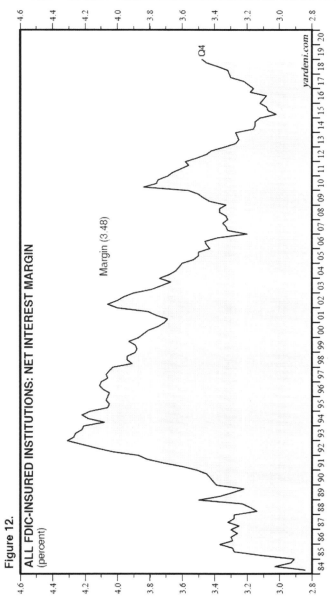

Figure 12.

ALL FDIC-INSURED INSTITUTIONS: NET INTEREST MARGIN
(percent)

Margin (3.48)

Q4

Source: Federal Deposit Insurance Corporation, Quarterly Banking Profile.

yardeni.com

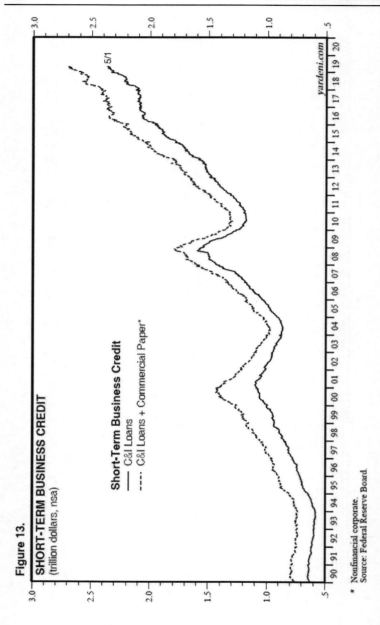

Figure 13.

SHORT-TERM BUSINESS CREDIT
(trillion dollars, nsa)

Short-Term Business Credit
— C&I Loans
--- C&I Loans + Commercial Paper*

* Nonfinancial corporate.
Source: Federal Reserve Board

yardeni.com

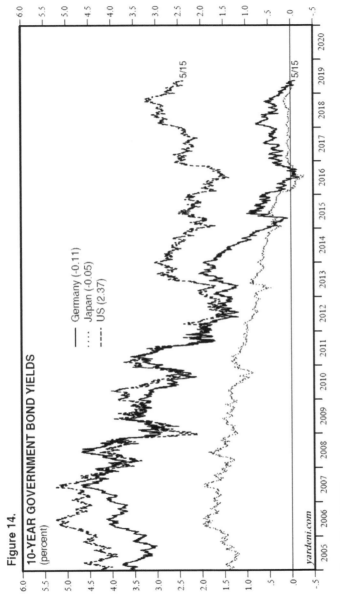

Figure 14.

10-YEAR GOVERNMENT BOND YIELDS
(percent)

Germany (-0.11)
Japan (-0.05)
US (2.37)

yardeni.com

Source: Haver Analytics.

Figure 15.

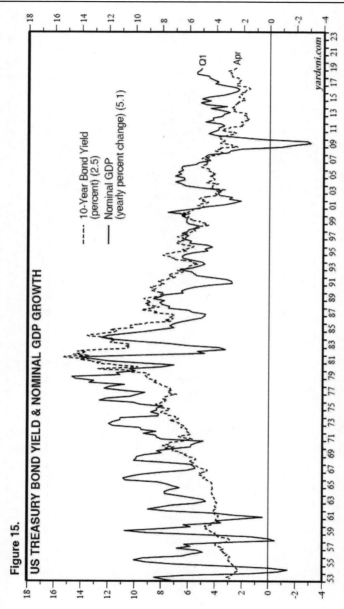

US TREASURY BOND YIELD & NOMINAL GDP GROWTH

---- 10-Year Bond Yield
(percent) (2.5)

—— Nominal GDP
(yearly percent change) (5.1)

Q1

Apr

yardeni.com

Source: Bureau of Economic Analysis and Federal Reserve Board.

Figure 16.

SPREAD BETWEEN US TREASURY BOND YIELD & NOMINAL GDP GROWTH*
(percentage points)

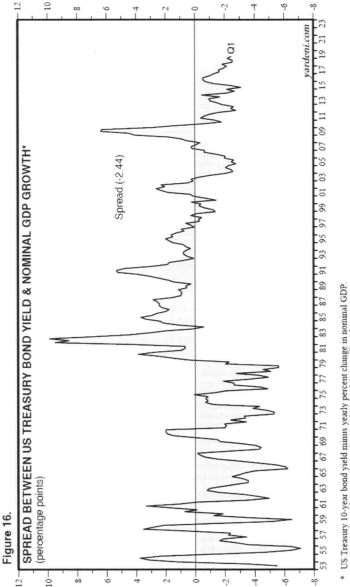

Spread (-2.44)

Q1

yardeni.com

* US Treasury 10-year bond yield mnms yearly percent change in nominal GDP.
Source: Bureau of Economic Analysis and Federal Reserve Board.

Figure 17.

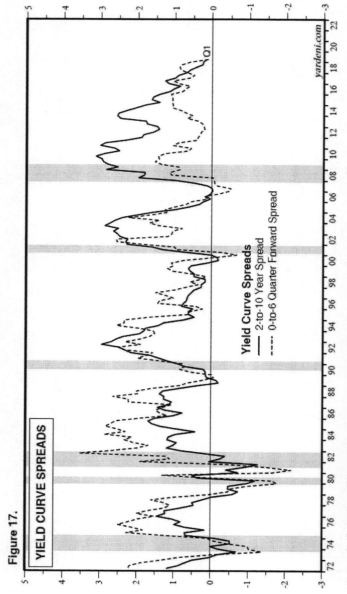

YIELD CURVE SPREADS

Yield Curve Spreads
— 2-to-10 Year Spread
--- 0-to-6 Quarter Forward Spread

yardeni.com

* Data for Q1-2019 is an FRB estimate based on data through January.
Note: Shaded areas denote recessions according to the National Bureau of Economic Research.
Source: Federal Reserve Board.

Figure 18.

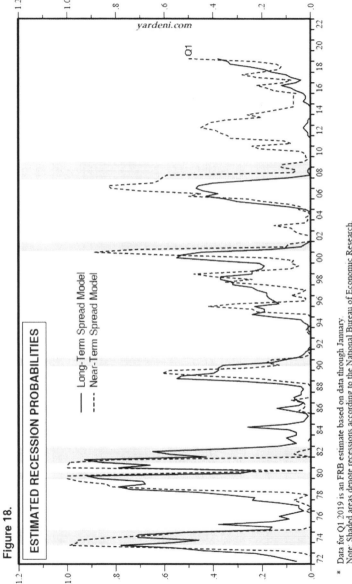

ESTIMATED RECESSION PROBABILITIES

—— Long-Term Spread Model
----- Near-Term Spread Model

yardeni.com

* Data for Q1 2019 is an FRB estimate based on data through January.
Note: Shaded areas denote recessions according to the National Bureau of Economic Research.
Source: Federal Reserve Board

Figure 19.

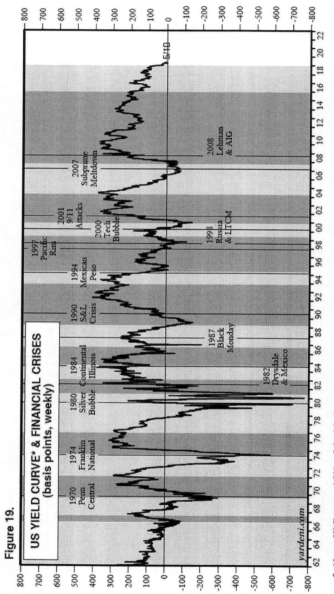

US YIELD CURVE* & FINANCIAL CRISES
(basis points, weekly)

* 10-year US Treasury yield less federal funds rate.
Note: Dark grey shaded areas denote periods of monetary easing between cyclical peaks and troughs in the federal funds rate. Light grey shaded areas denote monetary tightening periods.
Source: Federal Reserve Board.

Figure 20.

2-YEAR TREASURY NOTE YIELD & FEDERAL FUNDS RATE FUTURES
(percent)

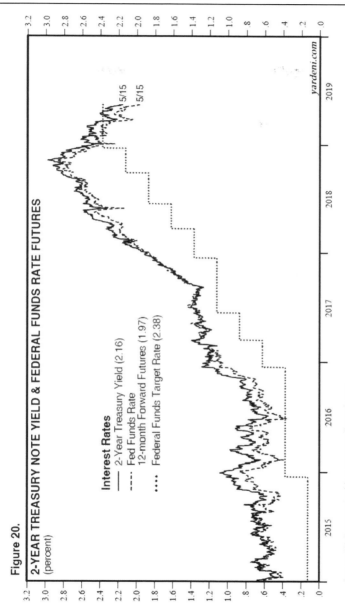

Interest Rates
— 2-Year Treasury Yield (2.16)
- - - Fed Funds Rate
- - - 12-month Forward Futures (1.97)
· · · Federal Funds Target Rate (2.38)

yardeni.com

Source: US Treasury & Chicago Mercantile Exchange.

Figure 21.

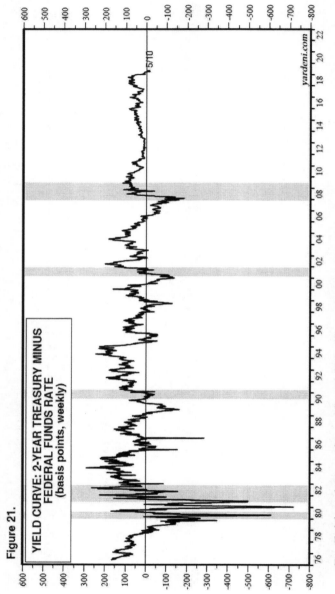

YIELD CURVE: 2-YEAR TREASURY MINUS
FEDERAL FUNDS RATE
(basis points, weekly)

Note: Shaded areas denote recessions according to the National Bureau of Economic Research.
* 2-year Treasury yield less federal funds rate.
Source: Board of Governors of the Federal Reserve System.

yardeni.com

Figure 22.

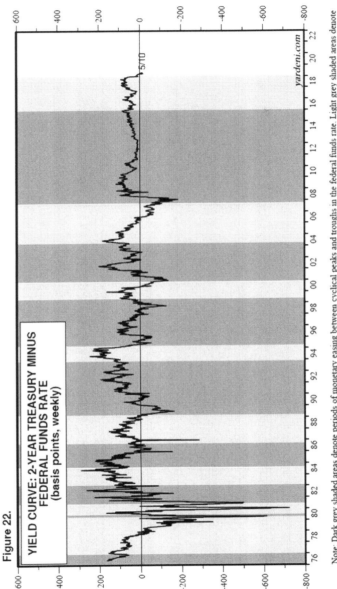

YIELD CURVE: 2-YEAR TREASURY MINUS
FEDERAL FUNDS RATE
(basis points, weekly)

Note: Dark grey shaded areas denote periods of monetary easing between cyclical peaks and troughs in the federal funds rate. Light grey shaded areas denote
monetary tightening periods.
* 2-year Treasury yield less federal funds rate.
Source: Board of Governors of the Federal Reserve System.

yardeni.com

36978260R00033